7.99
J394.261

DEC 0 1 2016

Winchester Public Library
Winchester, MA 01890
781-721-7171
www.winpublib.org

D1540490

CHINESE NEW YEAR

Michelle Lee

World's Greatest Celebrations: Chinese New Year

Copyright © 2017
Published by Scobre Educational
Written by Michelle Lee

All rights reserved.

Printed in the United States of America.

No part of this book may be reproduced in any manner whatsoever
without written permission, except in the case of brief quotations
embodied in critical articles and reviews.

Scobre Educational
42982 Osgood Road
Fremont, CA 94539

www.scobre.com
info@scobre.com

Scobre Educational publications may be purchased for
educational, business, or sales promotional use.

Cover and Layout by Sara Radka
Edited by Lauren Dupuis-Perez
Copyedited by Malia Green
Images sourced from iStock, Shutterstock, and Newscom

ISBN: 978-1-62920-567-0 (hardcover)
ISBN: 978-1-62920-566-3 (eBook)

TABLE OF CONTENTS

INTRODUCTION

Chinese New Year is a holiday that is celebrated in China and many other places in the world. While most of the world uses the Western calendar, the Chinese calendar is different because it is based on the cycles of the moon. This is why Chinese New Year is often called the **Lunar** New Year.

The Chinese New Year begins on the second **new moon** after the start of winter (December 21) and takes place in late January to early February. The celebration starts on Chinese New Year's Eve and ends during the Lantern festival. It is a 15-day-long event to celebrate change, new fortunes, and family.

The days before the New Year are already very busy. Chinese families may give their homes a full cleaning so that the bad luck can be swept away and their homes can be ready to receive good luck.

Red lanterns are an iconic decoration for Chinese New year. Here, they line a street in Sabah, Malaysia.

The Ke Lok Si Temple in Penang, Malaysia, is covered in festive lights in celebration of the Chinese New Year.

Streets are decorated in red and Chinese **scrolls** bearing lucky messages are hung upon doors and windows. On Chinese New Year's Eve, families celebrate with a large **reunion** dinner called *Nian Ye Fan*, or "Evening of the Passing Year." At the stroke of midnight, fireworks and firecrackers are lit.

The day of the New Year is about honoring family—especially one's elders—and one may spend the day visiting older members of the family. The streets are also crowded with lots of loud music and activities.

HISTORY

According to Chinese **mythology**, the New Year celebration began with a village's struggle against a monster named Nian. Half lion and half dragon, Nian would come down from the mountains every spring and eat the people inside the village. Frightened, the villagers would put food outside their doors each year to make Nian full so that he would not hurt them.

However, the monster returned year after year, and the people lived in great fear—until one New Year's Eve, an old, wise man travelled to the village. He saw the people's fearful faces and asked them why they were afraid when they should be celebrating the beginning of the New Year. The villagers told him of Nian and his yearly attacks. The old man told them that he would help them, but the villagers thought he was crazy and ignored him.

When nightfall came, everyone except the old man left the village to escape the monster.

Nian is a legendary Chinese monster that is half lion and half dragon.

Furong Zhen is a traditional Chinese mountain village in Hunan Province.

When Nian came down to the village, he tore through every house—searching for people and eating the food that the villagers had left for him. But as Nian made his way to the last house, he was blinded by the shining red paper and bright lights of the candles that decorated the outside. The old man soon burst through the house's doors and shouted at the monster while firecrackers exploded and snapped behind him. Frightened by the sights and the noises, Nian ran away and returned to the mountains.

The next day, the people returned to the village and were surprised to see that the old man was still alive. The old man then told them about the monster's weaknesses. The next year, the villagers began decorating their homes with red lanterns and scrolls, dressing up in red, and making loud noises and bright lights to scare Nian away. After the villagers started doing this, Nian stopped coming to the village.

Bright lights and the color red are some of Nian's weaknesses.

But, knowing that the monster was still alive and might still come back, the villagers continued their **tradition** of scaring Nian away. This tradition eventually spread to all of China and still continues today.

Chinese New Year has also faced some changes throughout the centuries. During the rule of the Communist leader Mao Tse-tung (1945-1976), Chinese New Year was not allowed to be celebrated, and the Western calendar was closely followed. After Mao, however, Chinese leaders brought the tradition back and declared Chinese New Year a national holiday.

During this time, Chinese citizens take a week-long vacation to celebrate and spend time with their families. Chinese New Year's name has also changed. Its traditional name was *Nian jie*, or New Year Festival, but now its modern name is *Chun jie*, or Spring Festival.

Some Chinese New Year traditions have also changed. In the past, family reunion dinners took place at home. Today, more and more Chinese families eat out at restaurants and hotels for the New Year. Fireworks have also become a large safety and **pollution** concern, so there are not as many fireworks as there used to be.

Fireworks in celebration of Chinese New Year

Chinese New Year takes place during the spring. In this picture, the women are dressed up as flowers to celebrate the new season.

Traditionally, New Year's greetings were spoken in person. Today, more people are using other ways to send their greetings, whether it is through telephone, e-mail, or the internet. They also spend their time watching the *Spring Festival Gala*, a popular TV show with musical and dramatic performances.

Chinese New Year masks are usually very bright and colorful. They show people's happiness and excitement for the festival.

THE COLORS OF CHINESE NEW YEAR

Red is the color you will see the most during Chinese New Year because it wards off evil spirits like Nian. In Chinese culture, red represents good luck and happiness.

Green represents spring, money, and health.

Yellow represents royalty.

LOCATION

Some Chinese folktales say that the dragon has all the characteristics of the 12 zodiac animals. For example, this dragon has the teeth of a tiger, the whiskers of a rat, the nose of a pig, and the body of a snake.

China is the most populated country in the world, so Chinese New Year is the world's biggest celebration. Although less **superstitious** now, China is still a culture that respects and celebrates old traditions. For example, people still take the **zodiac signs** very seriously.

In Chinese culture, the 12 zodiac signs are all animals. They are very important to the Chinese calendar, so each Chinese New Year celebrates a different animal. The animals are organized in a specific order: rat, ox, tiger, rabbit, dragon, snake, horse, ram, monkey, rooster, dog, and pig. Dragons are one of the most important animals because it is believed that Chinese people are related to dragons. Thus, dragons are lucky and can often be seen in New Year parades.

The rabbit is also an important animal because of its connection to the moon goddess, Chang'E. When Chang'E floated to the moon and became a goddess, it is said that she brought a rabbit to keep her company. During the Lantern Festival (the last day of Chinese New Year), people light up lanterns in the shape of rabbits.

Rabbit lanterns parade through the streets during Hong Kong's Lantern Festival.

DID YOU KNOW?

One Chinese tradition is to put away sharp objects during the first few days of the Chinese New Year Festival. The superstition is that sharp objects like knives and scissors could cut away good luck.

MEANING

The original meaning behind Chinese New Year was religious. It was a celebration of the monster Nian's defeat and a time to honor the gods. Houses were cleaned before the New Year so that they could be ready for a visit from the gods, and **incense** and food were left out as offerings. While some of these traditions still continue today, Chinese New Year has changed to a more family-based celebration. It is a time to reconnect with relatives, honor one's elders, and show kindness with gift-giving.

Food and incense are left in shrines as offerings to the Chinese gods and ancestors.

Chinese New Year is all about spending time with family and sharing gifts.

Chinese families may also prepare for the New Year by making **resolutions** such as getting haircuts, replacing broken items, finishing school work, or ending arguments and fights. Just like the New Year celebrated in the West, Chinese New Year is about letting go of all the bad things in the past and making changes to become a better person.

DID YOU KNOW?

Gifts have special meaning during Chinese New Year. Sweet gifts like candy and cake will sweeten someone's year. Orchids bring good luck and bamboo plants represent strength. Giving someone lotus or watermelon seeds will multiply their fortunes. Nian gao—a traditional rice cake from southern China— is another very popular gift item. The rice cakes are very sticky, reminding people of the importance of sticking together with friends and family.

SPECIAL EVENTS

There are many events that take place during the New Year celebration. On New Year's Eve, people have *Nian Ye Fan* (a family reunion dinner) and then stay up until midnight to welcome the New Year. On New Year's Day, Chinese gods and ancestors are honored.

Family altars are lit with candles and incense. Food is also left on the altar so that the gods and ancestor spirits can have something to eat. On this day, families also make trips to visit distant relatives and *lai see* (red envelopes filled with money) are given as gifts.

Throughout the 15-day celebration, there are dragon and lion dances, drum and gong contests, parades, costumes, operas and dramas acted out on the streets, and acrobatic shows. The most popular performance is the dragon dance. A long, handmade dragon is carried by dancing performers.

During Chinese New Year, people light up incense (scented sticks) as offerings to gods and ancestors.

The Dragon Dance Show is performed in Taipei, Taiwan.

The dancers twist and turn the dragon to copy the movement of a river. In Chinese mythology, the dragon is a friendly water creature that brings good luck to the community. The longer the dragon, the more luck it will bring.

DID YOU KNOW?

According to *The Guinness Book of World Records*, the longest Chinese dragon danced in Markham, Ontario, Canada, on September 30, 2012. The dragon was more than 18,269 feet long, and was carried by over 3,000 people.

WHAT SETS IT APART

Chinese New Year is more than 3,000 years old. It takes place during China's springtime, in January or February. Since China is mostly a farming country, the people pay great attention to the seasons and times of harvesting and planting. Chinese New Year is the time of new seeds and new beginnings. Farmers celebrate their hard work from last year and pray for another good harvest to come.

Springtime in China.

The tradition spread to other regions as people left the country and formed cities. Today, it is even more mainstream as Chinese communities across the world unite for this celebration each year. Other countries with large Chinese New Year celebrations include Taiwan, Singapore, Macau, Thailand, Malaysia, the United States, and the Philippines.

The streets are decorated for Chinese New Year in San Francisco.

DID YOU KNOW?

With nearly one million people each year, the biggest celebration outside of China occurs in San Francisco's Chinatown.

HIGHLIGHTS

LAI SEE

Lai see are money gifts given in celebration of the New Year. The money comes in red envelopes because red is the color that Nian is afraid of. Thus, *lai see* ward off evil spirits and bring good luck to the people that receive them. Traditionally, it is married people who give *lai see* and unmarried people like children who receive them. *Lai see* can also be given as tips or thank-you gifts to lion-dance performers, teachers, or other members of the community. In honor of the New Year, the red envelopes are filled with new, crisp dollars.

CCTV'S *SPRING FESTIVAL GALA*

The *Spring Festival Gala* is a TV show that takes place on Chinese New Year's Eve and ends with a countdown to the New Year. Celebrities from China and around the world get together and perform. It is a show where performers wear traditional clothing, fancy costumes, and bright red colors. Some performers even dress up as the zodiac animal of that year.

Music and dance make up most of the show. It features both traditional and modern Chinese music, as well as some popular songs from other countries. The show can also be educational, with scenes showing how Chinese New Year is celebrated. Hosts also talk about the importance of spending time with family, doing well in school, and helping others in the community. In addition to these performances, the show has many comedy dramas, acrobats, and even magic shows.

THE ANIMAL ZODIAC

The Animal Zodiac is important to Chinese New Year because it has been used as a way of recording time for thousands of years. Chinese years are associated with one of 12 different animals. These animals come from ancient folktales and stories that have been used to give valuable lessons and guidance to Chinese children.

Each animal has its own personality which can be used to figure out what kind of year the next one will be. For example, the Year of the Ox can be a good, strong year because the ox is a strong animal. But it can also be a difficult year, since the ox is thought to be very stubborn. Children born under these animal years are also believed to have specific personality traits.

Want to know your zodiac animal and personality?
Find the animal for the year you were born:

Year of the Rat: 1948, 1960, 1972, 1984, 1996, 2008, 2020
Personality: Rats are charming, adventurous, and smart, but also very picky.

Year of the Ox: 1949, 1961, 1973, 1985, 1997, 2009, 2021
Personality: Oxen are strong, patient, and independent, but sometimes too stubborn.

Year of the Tiger: 1938, 1950, 1962, 1974, 1986, 1998, 2010
Personality: Tigers are powerful, brave, and kind, but sometimes overreact to small situations.

Year of the Rabbit: 1939, 1951, 1963, 1975, 1987, 1999, 2011
Personality: Rabbits are kind, friendly, and creative, but also very shy.

Year of the Dragon: 1940, 1952, 1964, 1976, 1988, 2000, 2012
Personality: Dragons are strong, independent, and generous, but can easily be discouraged.

Year of the Snake: 1941, 1953, 1965, 1977, 1989, 2001, 2013
Personality: Snakes are charming, wise, and graceful, but can sometimes be greedy.

Year of the Horse: 1942, 1954, 1966, 1978, 1990, 2002, 2014
Personality: Horses are popular, energetic, and strong, but sometimes cause tantrums when things don't go their way.

Year of the Ram: 1943, 1955, 1967, 1979, 1991, 2003, 2015
Personality: Rams are artistic, caring, and trustworthy, but have a habit of spending money on things that they don't need.

Year of the Monkey: 1944, 1956, 1968, 1980, 1992, 2004, 2016
Personality: Monkeys are charming, clever, and talented, but often mischievous.

Year of the Rooster: 1945, 1957, 1969, 1981, 1993, 2005, 2017
Personality: Roosters are hard-working, ambitious, and organized, but can sometimes be very selfish.

Year of the Dog: 1946, 1958, 1970, 1982, 1994, 2006, 2018
Personality: Dogs are kind, loyal, and caring, but often impatient.

Year of the Pig: 1947, 1959, 1971, 1983, 1995, 2007, 2019
Personality: Pigs are kind, strong, and honest, but too trusting of others.

AROUND THE WORLD

The Chinese New Year celebration in **San Francisco, California**, is the largest Asian event in the United States. There is a large parade filled with red and gold floats, lion dancers, firecrackers, school marching bands, acrobats, and martial artists. At night, the Golden Dragon is awakened.

The **River Hong Bao** is a large Chinese New Year carnival. The night is lit up by gigantic lanterns of Chinese gods, legendary heroes, and the 12 zodiac animals. There are performances by the Yunnan Opera Theatre and fancy foods to eat like vanilla rice, spicy fishballs, and quail eggs.

In the **Philippines**, the Chinese community celebrates with fireworks, dragons, and red envelopes. Houses are cleaned and candy is thrown onto the streets to attract good spirits. Some Chinese and Filipino traditions have joined together such as eating of *suha* (a local fruit similar to grapefruit) and *hopia* (a round, sweet cake).

In **Miaoli, Taiwan**, there is a New Year tradition called "Bombing the Dragon." During the Lantern Festival, people throw firecrackers at the dancing dragons. The tradition started because it used to be very hard to see the dragons at night and the firecrackers helped by lighting up everything. The colors and explosions make this a very magical night.

THE PEOPLE

In China, more than one billion people celebrate Chinese New Year. As workers hurry to get back home, travelling becomes a big hassle. Chinese citizens struggle to get train tickets, often waiting in lines for several hours. Stations become so crowded that just riding a bus or train can take close to a whole day. This shows how important Chinese New Year is to people and their families. Large crowds and long distances will not stop people from making the difficult journey back home.

Families usually celebrate Chinese New Year by staying at home and having a large, family dinner with homemade food. However, more families are beginning to eat out at restaurants with their friends. Many celebrities celebrate Chinese New Year by showing up and performing at the *Spring Festival Gala*. Action movie star Jackie Chan, pop singer Sun Nan, and magician Lu Chen are regulars on the show. In recent years, S.H.E., Celine Dion, Lee Min Ho (*Boy Over Flowers, City Hunter*), and Sophie Marceau (*Braveheart, The World is Not Enough*) have also made guest appearances.

DID YOU KNOW?

With more than 3 billion trips per year, Chinese New Year travel is the world's largest human **migration**.

Dancers perform the Thousand-handed Goddess of
Mercy dance on CCTV's Spring Festival Gala show.

IMPACT

China is a very popular destination during the New Year. According to *China Daily*, the capital city of Beijing received 9.75 million sightseers and $723 million in tourist sales. Chinese New Year brings great wealth to the country.

Tourists must be prepared for many businesses to be closed for several days in celebration. Most of China is cold at this time, so it is important to pack winter clothes, since shopping centers may not be open. Restaurants and grocery stores are still open, but their hours are limited. Even so, it is still worth it to watch the street parades, dragon and lion dances, and the spectacular firework shows in the public squares.

Most families spend their New Year at home or in the countryside, so it is a great time to visit normally crowded cities like Shanghai. Popular places like The Bund and the Shanghai Museum are still open throughout the festival. There is a lot to do at night as well. Even though most people are inside their homes, festival lights are turned on at night. It is very breathtaking to take a stroll through the cities and see the bright decorations and animal-shaped lanterns. Chinese New Year is a beautiful celebration that continues to bring family, friends, and learners of Chinese culture together.

迎春接福

Ying chun jie fu!

Welcome to the New Year and may you receive
much happiness and good fortune to come!

GLOSSARY

ancestor: a person far back in the family tree, such as a great-grandparent or forefather

incense: scented sticks that are burned to make sweet smells

lunar: an adjective that describes the moon

migration: a large movement of people or animals from one location to another

mythology: a set of stories belonging to a culture; usually about gods and heroes

new moon: a time when the moon is invisible in the night sky (a moonless night)

pollution: when the Earth gets very dirty from trash and other harmful objects

resolution: a decision or promise to do something

reunion: a gathering of family or friends after a long time of being apart

scroll: a long piece of paper. Scrolls usually have lucky messages written on them in Chinese.

superstition: a belief that is not based on reason or scientific knowledge

superstitious: an adjective that describes someone who believes in superstitions

tradition: a set of beliefs and practices that are passed down from generation to generation

zodiac: a collection of stars in the sky

zodiac sign: the zodiac is divided into 12 parts and each part is called a zodiac sign